Creating A Better Life
Three Keys To Possessing Your Destiny

Workbook

Creating a Better Life: Three Keys to Possessing Your Destiny Workbook
Published by Guy Thing Press
P.O. Box 827
Roanoke, TX 76262

This book or parts thereof may not be reproduced in any form, stored in a retrieval system, or transmitted in any form by any means - electronic, mechanical, photocopy, recording, or otherwise - without prior written permission of the publisher, except as provided by United States of America copyright law.

Guy Thing Press books my be purchased in bulk for educational, business, fund-raising, or sales promotional use. For more information, please contact Guy Thing Press.

Please visit us at www.guythingpress.com

Copyright © 2008 by Guy Thing Press
All Rights Reserved

Printed in the United States of America

ISBN-13: 978-0-9818337-1-2
ISBN-10: 0-9818337-1-3

Scripture taken from the New King James Version. Copyright © 1982 by Thomas Nelson, Inc. Used by permission. All rights reserved.

Contents

Lesson One: As A Man Thinks, So He Is 1

Lesson Two: Rekindle Vision for Life. 7

Lesson Three: Go In! Don't Walk In Circles 13

Lesson Four: A Broad Foundation 19

Lesson Five: Key Number One: What's In Your Mouth 23

Lesson Six: Think And Do. Keys Three And Two 29

Lesson Seven: Words Of Authority 35

Lesson Eight: Create And Sustain 41

Lesson Nine: The Power Of An Image 47

Lesson Ten: Destroyed By An Image 53

Lesson Eleven: Close Down The Pool 59

Lesson One
As A Man Thinks, So He Is

Creating a Better Life

1. You can't be anything other than _____

2. You can always hide the real you.

    True   False

3. Sometimes you can learn more about a person in a _____ of time than you have learned about him in years, when that person has let his _____ _____, just for an instant.

4. Who is the real man?

    The Inner Man   The Outer Man

5. All mistakes in life come from wrong _____. Wrong _____ produces wrong _____. All wrong _____ are based on wrong _____. Wrong _____ cannot produce _____ _____.

6. Who has the ability to control your thoughts?

    _____

7. Who has authority and power over your thinking?

    _____

   1 Corinthians 2:14-16

   But the natural man does not receive the things of the Spirit of God, for they are foolishness to him; nor can he know them, because they are spiritually discerned. But he who is spiritual judges all things, yet he himself is rightly judged by no one. For "who has known the mind of the LORD that he may instruct Him?" But we have the mind of Christ.

8. As Christians, we should have the mind of _____.

Lesson 1
As A Man Thinks, So He Is

9. God thinks like we do.

   True   False

10. God's thoughts and His ways _____ ours, and at the point of confrontation, bring us to a time of _____.

   Romans 12: 2

   Do not be conformed to this world, but be transformed by the renewing of your mind, that you may prove (demonstrate, display, manifest) what is that good and acceptable and perfect will of God.

11. God's will for us is _____, _____, and _____.

12. Explain what God's will is NOT:

   _____

   _____

   _____

   Jesus didn't come to give us a pathetic life, a mediocre life, an average life, a fairly good life, or just a good life…He came to give us better than that…a better life…the abundant life.

13. The Bible says that we can be _____ by the renewing, the remaking of our mind.

14. We need to replace _____ _____ with _____ _____, our thoughts with _____ _____.

Creating a Better Life

Lesson 1
As A Man Thinks, So He Is

Key Point Review

1. We are what we _____.

2. What we think _____ who we are, what we do, and what we have.

3. Wrong thinking produces wrong _____, and wrong results.

4. Only _____ have the power to control our thoughts.

5. We have the power to choose what we think and _____.

6. God does not think like we think. His thoughts are _____ than ours.

7. We can _____, that is, make new our minds, making new what we think, so that we can have what God wants us to have, and what we also really want for our lives, the better life, the abundant life.

Lesson Two
Rekindle Vision for Life

Creating a Better Life

1. How does a person drown?

    A. By falling in water

    B. By staying in water

2. You have time and can _____ your _____ around with God's help. He is not against you. God is with you!

3. How do you measure true success?
_____

4. Was heaven created for the scholarly elite?
_____

5. _____ led the nation of Israel, the people of Israel, several million of them, out of 400 years of a life of slavery and servitude in the land of Egypt.

6. While living as a prince in Pharaoh's court, he observed an Egyptian abusing a Hebrew, and in the effort to defend the Hebrew he _____ the Egyptian.

7. Moses thought by killing the Egyptian he was doing what was _____, _____, _____.

8. Instead, it produced _____

9. As a result of Moses' wrong thinking, and his wrong actions, he was forced to flee to the _____ regions, where he eventually married, and spent _____ years tending his father in law's sheep.

10. God called Moses to come out of the _____, to go to Pharaoh to persuade him to let the nation of God's people be _____ into freedom and a better life.

11. Did Moses have confidence in himself when God, through the burning bush, called him? What

Lesson 2
Rekindle Vision For Life

were some of the excuses he gave? How did God respond?

_____

_____

_____

12. Based on the previous question, why shouldn't God rekindle long buried aspirations, dreams, visions, and hopes, regardless of how long it's been since they've seem the light of day in your own life?

_____

_____

_____

Isaiah 9: 6-7

For unto us a Child is born, unto us a Son is given; And the government will be upon His shoulder,.... of the increase of His government and peace, THERE WILL BE NO END...

13. A characteristic of the government of the Kingdom of God is ever increasing _____, _____, _____, and _____.

Psalms 115:12-15

The Lord has been mindful of us; He will bless us; He will bless the house of Israel; He will bless the house of Aaron. He will bless those who fear the Lord, both small and great. May the Lord give you increase MORE AND MORE, you and your children. May you be blessed by the Lord, who made heaven and earth.

Creating a Better Life

Lesson 2
Rekindle Vision For Life

Key Point Review:

1. Even seemingly _____ ideas of our own, can have unexpected, even disastrous consequences. Good ideas are not necessarily "God Ideas".

2. The Kingdom of God operates simply. _____ can understand it if they make the effort.

3. True success is not measured by what you've done, but by what you've done compared to what _____ _____ _____.

4. A person doesn't drown by falling into water. He drowns by _____ there.

5. _____, _____, _____ give up or quit on your life, on your dreams.

6. Say _____ to rekindling dreams for your life, whether they be new dreams or resurrected ones.

7. Continual increase (growth) is a characteristic of _____ kingdom. It is therefore a characteristic of each member in that kingdom. He will increase us more and more.

Lesson Three
Go In! Don't Walk In Circles

Creating a Better Life

1. How many days should the journey across the wilderness have been?

    A. One

    B. Three

    C. Seven

    D. Forty

2. How many spies were sent in to assess the Promised Land?

    A. One

    B. Two

    C. Seven

    D. Twelve

3. Upon their return, the spies confirmed indeed it was a rich, fertile, land…a land of milk and honey….milk meaning _____ and new life, and honey meaning a _____ life.

4. God loves to show us appetizers! Appetizers help build a _____ of what God has waiting for us.

5. What is the price for a mediocre life?

_____

6. What is the price for a great life?

_____

7. _____ spies gave a bad report, and only _____ spies gave a good report.

Lesson 3
Go In! Don't Walk In Circles

8. The majority is often _____. Why?

_____

_____

_____

9. This majority is not always out in the _____ world, it can also be found in the _____, among God's own people.

10. If you are to get anywhere in life with God, you must learn to _____ _____ with God.

11. There will always be _____ and _____ between those who dare to believe God's promises for their lives, and those who find them too challenging, or those who simply don't believe in them at all.

12. We must be so careful about what we _____ about God, and be even more careful about what we _____.

13. There will always be _____ standing between you and God's promises for your life.

James 1:6

"...he who doubts is like the wave of the sea, driven and tossed by the wind. For let not that man think he will receive ANYTHING from the Lord; he is a double minded man, unstable in all his ways."

14. When we treat God's word with contempt or disrespect, we do so at our own _____.

Creating a Better Life

Lesson 3
Go In! Don't Walk In Circles

Key Point Review:

1. There will always be _____ or _____ standing between you and God's promises for your life.

2. Some _____ can take on giant proportions.

3. The old way of life will always _____ you until you drown it out of existence and never look back.

4. The majority is often _____, heads in the _____ direction and talks ten times as much.

5. At times we must learn to _____ _____ with our God.

6. A _____ _____ man should not think he will get anything from our Lord.

7. Don't spend your life walking around in _____ settling for the same old manna.

Lesson Four
A Broad Foundation

Creating a Better Life

1. In order to possess the promises God has for us, we must understand the general requirements for the _____ of the conquest.

2. Who guarantees the results?

_____

3. We will always need _____ strategies for _____ "conquests" in our lives, but the overall _____ upon which all the _____ conquests rests needs to be in place first.

4. God will give each one of us foundational _____, foundational _____, that are the _____ for our destiny in Him.

> *Joshua 1:7-8*
>
> *Only be strong and very courageous, that you may observe to do according to all the law which Moses My servant commanded you; do not turn from it to the right hand or to the left, that you may prosper wherever you go.*
>
> *This Book of the Law shall not depart from your mouth, but you shall meditate in it day and night, that you may observe to do according to all that is written in it. For then you will make your way prosperous, and then you will have good success.*

5. Here, God was showing His people, and Joshua the leader of the people, the _____ _____, the _____ strategy for successfully possessing their future, the destiny God had prepared for them.

6. The fact that Moses could not lead Israel into the land God promised them makes him a poor leader.

    True   False

7. Some churches and ministries can get you saved, they can lead you out of _____ from the life of sin, the life of mediocrity. But, that doesn't mean they can lead you _____; lead you in to the _____ of the life God has promised.

Lesson 4
A Broad Foundation

Key Point Review:

1. God wants us to _____ the big _____ of a life with Him at the center.

2. God can and will speak to you through His _____, if you take the time to look there.

3. God has already given the _____ _____, guaranteed by Him personally, to bring us to posses the life of our dreams.

4. God will give us the foundational _____, the principle _____ that serve as the _____ of our personal destiny in Him.

5. Not all _____ can lead you in to _____ the life God has planned for you. Some can only get you _____.

Lesson Five
Key Number One: What's In Your Mouth

Creating a Better Life

1. Why don't some Christians reach God's promises?

_____

_____

_____

2. Where are many people content to live?

_____

_____

_____

3. Good is often the enemy of _____.

4. What is the worth of _____, if its cost is missing God's _____?

5. Take an inventory of the dream in your own heart. What is the condition of that dream?

_____

_____

_____

6. There will always be _____ naysayers to every Joshua and Caleb who dares to believe God.

Lesson 5
Key Number One: What's In Your Mouth

Joshua 1:7-8

Only be thou strong and very courageous, that you may observe to do according to all the law which Moses My servant commanded you; do not turn from it to the right hand or to the left, that you may prosper wherever you go.

This book of the law shall not depart from your mouth, but you shall meditate in it day and night, that you may observe to do according to all that is written in it. For then you will make your way prosperous, and then you will have good success

7. How many times does God tell Joshua to be strong and courageous in the book of Joshua chapter one?

   A. One

   B. Three

   C. Too many to count

8. If we are to possess our promises, our destiny, there will be _____, there will be _____, and there will be _____ _____.

9. What three things did God expect from Joshua?

   _____

   _____

   _____

10. Key number one: speak only what _____ _____.

25

Lesson 5
Key Number One: What's In Your Mouth

Key Point Review:

1. Surround yourself with _____ people.

2. The _____ zone is not where your promised life can be found.

3. _____ is often the enemy of _____, and great the enemy of _____.

4. Make your life count for something _____ than yourself.

5. There will always be _____ naysayers, and the noise of the crowd, for every Joshua and Caleb that dares to believe God, whether you are a _____ or a _____.

6. Three character qualities are required to enter into God's promised life, _____, _____, _____.

7. Don't _____ with God. The only thing in your mouth should be what God _____.

Lesson Six
Think And Do, Keys Three And Two

Creating a Better Life

1. You must learn to think like _____ _____.

2. Having God's _____ serves as a source of strength when the voices of negativity are not only all around us, but raging _____ us as well.

3. Many times in life people _____ in the "battlefield of the mind", before the _____ appears in their _____.

4. Truth is a powerful _____ and a powerful _____.

Malachi 3:6

I am the Lord, I do not change.

5. God cannot, and will not, _____ His _____ to meet ours. We must _____ our _____ to conform to His.

6. God's will for us is _____, _____, and _____.

7. How do we demonstrate faith?

_____

_____

_____

8. Speaking God's _____, His _____ the foundation of our thought life and our thought processes, and then _____ upon what we know, will produce visible results in our lives, results that we and others can see.

9. What will children reproduce?

_____

Lesson 6
Think And Do, Keys Three And Two

10. What one thing does anointing require?

_____

11. What is one of the greatest needs in the church today?

_____

12. What are some of the reasons why businesspeople are not involved in church?

_____

_____

_____

Deuteronomy 8:18

And you shall remember the LORD your God, for it is He who gives you power to get wealth, that He may establish His covenant which He swore to your fathers, as it is this day.

13. Why has God given us the power to obtain wealth according to this verse?

_____

_____

_____

14. People will gladly pay for something of no value.

    True   False

15. In the culture of the United States, the church in many areas has been judged as _____, _____, and _____ with the human condition in the twenty first century.

16. The last thing the devil wants is a _____ _____ _____ that has the funds and resources to spread the gospel in its community, in its nation, and around the world.

17. The instructions we follow today, create the _____, the _____, and the _____ life we will walk in tomorrow.

18. What are some reasons why you may not see the power of God in your life?

_____

_____

_____

19. What is key number Three?

_____

Lesson 6
Think And Do, Keys Three And Two

Key Point Review:

1. Surround yourself with can do people. Stay away from _____.

2. God expects us to be _____, _____, and _____. Changes are often incremental, and consistency is vital.

3. Like Joshua, for us to take the land of promises for our lives, we must keep only His _____ in our mouths, His way of _____ in our mind, and conform our _____ to His guidelines for living in demonstration of what is _____ us. This is the formula

4. Joshua's adherence to God's instructions was confirmed by increase…increase in _____, increase in _____, increase in _____.

5. The last thing the devil wants is a _____ and _____ church that has the _____ and _____ to spread the _____, and impact _____.

6. If you will _____, _____, and _____ like God does, you will be in agreement with Him, and then you will make your way prosperous, and then you will have good success.

7. There is _____ in a transformed _____, transformed _____, and transformed _____.

Lesson Seven
Words Of Authority

Creating a Better Life

1. _____ and its quality, and _____, are in submission and subjection to the authority of the _____, and the _____.

2. Few of us fully understand the authority and power of our _____. If we did, we would change the way we _____.

3. What is the Hebrew word for "authority"?
_____

4. What other meanings does this word have?
_____

5. Where the word of a king is there is _____, and there is _____.

> *Revelation 5:9-10*
>
> *You were slain, and have redeemed us to God by Your blood out of every tribe and tongue and people and nation, and have made us kings and priests to our God; and we shall reign on the earth.*

6. Jesus redeemed us by His blood and made us _____ and _____.

7. If you don't think you are a _____, you _____ with God's _____.

8. There is no more powerful a word than the _____ word, because there is no higher authority than the _____.

9. God's house, a king's house, has protocol, royal protocol. We need to _____, _____, and _____ accordingly.

10. A King's words have more authority than the king.

    True   False

**Lesson 7
Words Of Authority**

Matthew 24:35

Heaven and earth will pass away, but my words will by no means pass away.

11. God's words have _____ authority.

12. In our lives, our _____ take on more _____ than we have.

13. Your words take on a life _____ than your own, because they can _____ others.

14. We cancel out our prayers by _____ words, _____ _____ words, and then _____ God when the answers don't appear.

Lesson 7
Words Of Authority

Key Point Review

1. Where the word of a king is, there is _____, power. We have been made _____ and _____, seated in Christ, at the right hand of power, the right hand of the Father, above all other powers or names, present or future. Therefore our _____ have the power and _____ of our position in them.

2. Our _____ have _____ for _____ or for _____, regardless of our _____.

3. Because we are _____, there is no higher power or greater authority in our lives than our own _____, except _____ word…because He is the King of Kings.

4. Our _____ can take on a _____ of their own, impacting our lives and our families for generations.

5. If we make wrong decrees, we must make _____ ones to blunt the damage potential of our earlier statements. But, there still may be trouble. Better to _____ what we say, speaking in wisdom, according to what _____ speaks.

6. Controlling the mouth can create as near a _____ life as we can experience on this earth.

7. Saying both negative and positive things indicates we are _____ minded and not in position to receive anything from God. This is a bad way to live!

Lesson Eight
Create And Sustain

Creating a Better Life

John 1:1-4

In the beginning was the Word, and the Word was with God, and the Word was God. He was in the beginning with God. All things were made through Him, and without Him nothing was made that was made. In Him was life, and the life was the light of men.

1. The Word was God's very mind _____ and _____.

2. Without a word _____ was created. _____ was created by a word, more specifically by THE Word, known by name as _____ _____.

3. Jesus is the revealed Son of God, the _____ of God, God Himself, and the source of all created _____, and all created _____.

4. Everything God created, He _____.

5. Why did God create in the way He did?

_____

_____

_____

6. God created what He observed.

    True   False

7. _____ embody and release the _____ power of God.

8. Our _____, too, just like His can release and set into motion _____ power.

9. Christ _____ all things by the word of His power.

Lesson 8
Create And Sustain

Amos 3:7

Surely the Lord GOD does nothing, unless He reveals His secret to His servants the prophets

10. Prophets are the _____ for God.

11. Just because there are Christians who become corrupt in their sin, or a pastor, or a prophet, or an evangelist who falls from grace through sin, does that invalidate God's giftings?

_____

_____

_____

12. Why should we not live in our past glory or experience?

_____

_____

_____

13. We need to employ an active strategy of _____, _____, and _____ God's will and destiny for us into existence.

Romans 10:9

That if you confess with your mouth the Lord Jesus and believe in your heart that God has raised Him from the dead, you will be saved.

For with the heart one believes unto righteousness, and with the mouth confession is made unto salvation.

14. List some areas of your life in which you can confess for salvation.

_____

_____

_____

15. If you're unhappy with any area of your life, _____ come up with a strategy of speaking, agreeing, and praying.

Mark 11:23

For assuredly, I say to you, whoever says to this mountain, "Be thou removed and cast into the sea," and does not doubt in his heart, but believes that those things he says will be done, he will have whatever he says.

16. Jesus does not say a person will have whatever he _____. He will only have whatever he _____ and _____.

17. We will be held accountable for every _____ word that comes forth from our mouths.

18. _____ is the key to _____. And _____ is the key to _____.

19. We as individuals don't _____ God because we really do not believe _____ leads to a better life.

Lesson 8
Create And Sustain

Key Point Review:

1. God, the Word, created all things through _____. Words embody the _____ power of God.

2. God, the Word, _____ all things through the word of His power. Words embody the sustaining power of God. If God _____ and _____ all things by His words, so should we by ours.

3. God will do _____ without revealing His will to His servants the _____, who will forthtell the mind and will of God.

4. With our heart we _____ God's promises and it is counted to us as righteousness, but with our mouth faith _____ of these promises must be made for our salvation in _____ area of our lives.

5. Don't wait for someone to go up to heaven, or someone to go down into the depths to bring _____ to life's challenges. Jesus already did it…now it is up to us to use the Word that's near us, even in our own mouth to address life's challenges.

6. We will be called into account for every _____ and _____ word we speak.

7. _____ is the key to prosperity. _____ is the key to obedience.

Lesson Nine
The Power Of An Image

Creating a Better Life

One of the most powerful things one can do in life is create an _____.

The power of an image can be _____ or _____.

The image we hold in our mind triggers automatic responses in our _____ and in our _____.

When comparing two people or products, our image of one may give it a higher status over the other. Does that make the one with a higher status the better choice? Explain.

_____

_____

_____

The image we hold in our mind may be _____ or it may be _____. Nevertheless, whatever it is will trigger automatic _____ and behavioral _____.

John 14:9

He who has seen Me has seen the Father.

If we want to see God, we need look no further than _____. He and the Father are _____.

The image we have of Jesus, or God, in our _____, determines how we _____ to Him, and how we respond to life's _____.

Only when we have the correct image of God, can we respond to him appropriately.

True   False

Lesson 9
The Power Of An Image

How can our image of God affect our worship of Him?

_____

_____

_____

How shall we truly know a Christian?

    A. Their talk

    B. Their reputation

    C. Their fruit

_____ may be one way, but the _____, the inner man, may be something totally different.

Lesson 9
The Power Of An Image

Key Point Review:

1. One of the most powerful things one can do is _____ an image.

2. The image we hold in our mind triggers automatic _____ in our thinking and our behavior.

3. The image in our mind can be _____ or _____, but it will still control responses in our _____ and _____.

4. Creating an accurate image of God in our mind will manifest in our _____ and our _____. We MUST CREATE an accurate image of God in our mind, if we are to inherit His _____.

5. Jesus is the express image of the _____. If you see Him, you see the _____.

6. All authority is given _____ on earth, and in heaven. There is no place His authority does not _____.

7. Faith, without working itself out in practical application to our daily lives, is _____, and indicates the image we hold of God in our minds, is one of a _____ God. It is the _____ image of God. We must create the _____ image of God.

Lesson Ten
Destroyed By An Image

Creating a Better Life

1. It is difficult for any group of people to rise above the leadership they _____ and _____ in, even if it is _____ leadership.

Numbers 13:27-28

We went to the land where you sent us. It truly flows with milk and honey, and this is its fruit. Nevertheless the people who dwell in the land are strong; the cities are fortified and very large; moreover we saw the descendants of Anak there. The Amalekites dwell in the land of the South; the Hittites, the Jebusites, and the Amorites dwell in the mountains; and the Canaanites dwell by the sea along the banks of the Jordan.

2. The tragedy of the Israelite's situation was not in the fact there were _____ in the land. God could do something about the giants. The tragedy was in what they _____ in themselves.

3. The Israelites, because of the way they _____, the way they _____, and the way they _____ would never manifest the _____ of God in their lives.

4. They never _____ for what God had _____ them.

5. The defeat was not inflicted upon them by an enemy from _____. It was inflicted by a deadlier enemy, the enemy _____.

6. They were defeated by the _____ of an image!

7. When we see ourselves in the image of a _____, the enemy of our souls sees it too, and _____ that we no longer are like the kings and queens we have in fact become, reigning and ruling in life, but like _____ that cannot be taken _____.

8. Meditation in the word is the process of tearing down _____ images, wrong thoughts, replacing them with correct _____ of who we are in God, and who He is to us.

9. Hearing the truth is not enough… _____ it is critical.

Lesson 10
Destroyed By An Image

2 Corinthians 10:3-5

For though we walk in the flesh, we do not war according to the flesh. For the weapons of our warfare are not carnal, but mighty in God for pulling down strongholds, casting down arguments, and every high thing that exalts itself against the knowledge of God, bringing every thought into captivity to the obedience of Christ.

10. The Israelites never _____ in the flesh. They never entered into a physical battle. They lost in the battlefield of the _____, defeated by an image, by _____ never brought captive to obedience.

11. Our weapons are not weapons of the _____. They are _____ weapons that pull down _____ in our minds, and in the spirit world.

12. Speak only what God says about _____, about _____, and about _____.

13. _____ and _____ only what God's word says about you, about life, about Himself.

14. _____ in daily life, what God says about you, what God says about life, and what God says about Himself.

Lesson 10
Destroyed By An Image

Key Point Review:

1. The tragedy in life is not always in what is _____ in the world around us, but in what is seen in _____.

2. Leaders in the church have a greater _____ for bringing the people into the land of promises for their lives. Woe unto the leaders that fail to do so. They will never enter in themselves.

3. The way we see _____ in life, and in Christ, will be the same way the _____ of our souls sees us.

4. We can be defeated in real life, by an _____ in our mind that is not real, is not true, and has no power other than what we ascribe to it.

5. Next to _____ an image, one of the most powerful things we can do in life is _____ an image. Some images need to be _____.

6. We have been given _____ to destroy wrong _____, and create new ones, the _____, _____, and _____.

7. _____ God's Word, _____ in God's Word, and _____ God's Word to our daily lives protects us from delusion and deception, while empowering us to possess the land of promise for our lives.

Lesson Eleven
Close Down The Pool

Creating a Better Life

1. Merely wanting to have a better life puts the responsibility on _____ _____.

2. Cooperating with God in creating a better life puts the responsibility where it ought to be, and that's on _____.

3. Cooperating with _____ in the process is work.

4. Why did the Great Society fail?

_____

_____

_____

5. We need to be _____ for a better life, not _____.

Galations 6: 7-9

Do not be deceived, God is not mocked; for whatever a man sows, that he will also reap....and let us not grow weary while doing good, for in due season we shall reap if we do not lose heart.

6. Sowing and doing good translate to the word _____. Plant _____, get _____.

7. When _____ showed up He didn't need to have the waters _____.

8. The crippled man responded to Jesus by saying, "I'm _____ for somebody to help me."

Lesson 11
Close Down The Pool

9. What excuses do we sometimes make to justify our not having a better life?

_____

_____

_____

10. God is not concerned with our _____. He's not even so much concerned with where we are _____. He knows the thoughts He has for us to give us a _____ and to give us a hope.

11. God is the God of the _____. He cares about our _____.

12. We don't need to wait until some angel, or some minister or prophet _____ the water and _____ us in.

13. All we need is _____.

14. Because you have _____ something and _____ it, you may still be a long ways away from _____ upon it.

15. All the others said He's a _____, He's a _____, but Peter said the words that can build a _____ and a _____.

16. If we have the Son of the Living God in us and working with us, _____ things are possible.

17. If we know the _____, the _____ is the only thing needed to set us _____ from our personal Egypt.

18. We need to leave behind limited _____, _____ mentality.

19. We need to possess in our _____ and _____, the true image of Jesus Christ, because He is the exact image and likeness of _____.

Lesson 11
Close Down The Pool

Think about what you have read and learned. What are the steps you need to take to start on your way to a better life. Maybe there are things you need to repent from. Write down your action plan that will take you from where you are now, to where God wants you to be.

_____

_____

_____

_____

_____

_____

_____

_____

_____

_____

Leaving those things behind, let's press on toward the mark of a higher calling and let's enjoy all the good things God has for us

Let the glory of God, even now, and even this week….. you let the glory of God fill your life. Welcome, to a better life.

God bless you richly, and increase you more and more! Amen and amen.

Resources of Interest

Character is King
Dr. John Binkley

It's a Guy Thing: Character is King takes you on your dream journey. There is a place called destiny that we all jouney to. We all have ideas, dreams and vision for what life should be. This book lays out a plan for that journey to realizing your dreams, to your destiny.

Let's Talk About Sex
Dr. John A. King

Let's face it. Sexuality is all around us. It's even on billboards, and television commercials. Sadly, It's a topic many men have to discover on their own because too many churches or pastors won't touch it. Let's Talk About Sex was written so men no longer have to discover the answers to the tough questions about sex on their own.

Now to Next
Dr. John A. King

What does the next generation church look like? Who are the people that will be involved in the next generation church? How will it come about?

Those are some of the questions answered in Dr. King's newest release, Now to Next: Blueprint for a Christian Revolution.

Helping Guys Become Men, Husbands, and Fathers
Dr. John A. King

It's a Guy Thing takes you on the journey of fatherhood. Dr. King shows you, in this book, the skills neccesary to become a good father. He shows you what can happen when a father is absent or simply not active in a child's life.
Being a male is a matter of birth. Being a man is a matter of choice. This book will help you make that choice.

To see all the titles available through Guy Thing Press, visit us online at www.guythingpress.com

Resources of Interest

Business By The Book
Dr. John A. King

The world's greatest handbook on leadership, economic and social excellence is not found in schoolbooks, but is Scripture. The principles in this book are tried, proven and resilient over centuries. Christ bet His life on it, and so can you.

Show Me the Money
Dr. John A. King

Time Magazine asked, "Does God want you to be rich?" The answer to that question is simply "No, God wants you to be *wealthy*." In *Show Me the Money*, you will learn the fundamentals of creating and using wealth in God's kingdom.

Achieving Authentic Wealth
Jeff McLoud

We need a vision that goes beyond our ability to be consumers only. A vision so big, so powerful, that we cannot even accomplish it in our own lifetime - a vision founded from the very heartbeat of God. We could see the vision fulfilled if we ask ourselves a simple question: "How can we achieve twice as much with half the money?"

Creating a Better Life
Erik A. Kudlis

In this easy to read manual, educator and administrator turned national and international businessman, Erik Kudlis, identifies three vital keys you must know and use, given by God Himself, that unlock the doors to the life God always wanted you to have.

To see all the titles available through Guy Thing Press, visit us online at www.guythingpress.com

Further Resources

The Godly Man Curriculum

The Godly Man Curriculum is the latest development of the International Men's Network. This training curriculum is designed to train men from all walks of life and give them a firm foundation of doctrine and Godly knowledge. This curriculum is available both over the internet for individual study or by DVD for seminars, Sunday schools, and men's meetings. With up to 7 hours of video teaching divided over numerous topics, the Godly Man Curriculum is an excellent tool that you can build your classes upon and grow yourself and your people.

Building Iron Men & Life As Leaders Networks

The Building Iron Men and Life as Leaders networks are two of IMN's finest resources. Each network provides you with a new teaching every month that will challenge and encourage you to grow. The Building Iron Men network features three teachings in both CD and DVD format that focus on your men, while the Life as Leaders network provides you with three CDs that teach you leadership principles you can use in every area of your life.

Both networks are phenomenal tools that are vital assets to any church and discipleship program.

For more information about these and other resources, visit us online at www.imnonline.org

Also check out these websites for great resources and training materials.

International Men's Network
www.imnonline.org

Guy Thing Press
www.guythingpress.com

The International Men's Network was founded by Dr. John A. King. Our purpose as an organization is to help men not only grow to become the leaders of their families and churches need, but also become men of God that make a lasting impact on those around them.

IMN is a missionary organization to the men of the world. We are committed to:

- Inspire all men to rise to a high standard of biblical manhood.
- Encourage them to excel in their roles as men, leaders, husbands, and fathers.
- Challenge them to be contributors to society and set an example based upon a biblical value system that will benefit this generation and lay a solid foundation for the next.

As an organization, the International Men's Network is dedicated to providing and hosting the best resources for men, whether it comes from teachings and lessons on CD/DVD format or via a conference that will teach men principles that will help them become more influential and effective in their lives.

For more information about IMN and its mission, visit us online at www.imnonline.org or contact us via phone at 817.993.0047

bringing a living Jesus to a dying world

The Christian Life Center was founded by Dr. John King and his wife, Beccy. With a vision to preach the gospel of Jesus Christ with unashamed passion and uncompromising truth, Christian Life Center aims to raise up the next generation of leaders to move into all the world and proclaim the truth of Christ to the lost and broken.

Located in the Keller, TX area, the Church sits in the prime location to reach the community and the people therein. The Church desires to give back to the community by providing outreaches to better and enrich its inhabitants. From kickboxing classes that are aimed at teaching children and adults self-defense to special service that commemorate and honor our country's war-time heroes, the church strives to bring a living Jesus to a dying world by new and imaginative means that will bless and change lives.

For more information about Christian Life Center and the resources it offers,
visit the website at www.clctx.org